# First World War
## and Army of Occupation
# War Diary
## France, Belgium and Germany

5 CAVALRY DIVISION
Headquarters, Branches and Services
Royal Army Ordnance Corps
Assistant Director Ordnance Services
1 January 1917 - 31 August 1917

WO95/1162/4

The Naval & Military Press Ltd
www.nmarchive.com
Published in association with The National Archives

Published by

## The Naval & Military Press Ltd

Unit 10 Ridgewood Industrial Park,

Uckfield, East Sussex,

TN22 5QE England

Tel: +44 (0) 1825 749494

www.naval-military-press.com

www.nmarchive.com

*This diary has been reprinted in facsimile from the original. Any imperfections are inevitably reproduced and the quality may fall short of modern type and cartographic standards.*

© **Crown Copyright**
**Images reproduced by permission of The National Archives, London, England, 2015.**

# Contents

| Document type | Place/Title | Date From | Date To |
|---|---|---|---|
| Heading | WO95/1162/4 | | |
| Heading | 5th Cavalry Division Dep. Asst Dir. Ord. Services Jan-Aug 1917 | | |
| Heading | War Diary of D.A.D.O.S. 5th Cavalry Division From 1st February 1917 To 31st January 1917 | | |
| War Diary | | 01/01/1917 | 31/08/1917 |

WO 95/1162/4

# 1917
## 5TH CAVALRY DIVISION

### DEP-ASST DIR. ORD. SERVICES
### JAN - AUG 1917

SERIAL NO. 305

# Confidential War Diary

OF

D.A.D.O.S., 5th CAVALRY DIVISION

FROM 1st February 1917 TO 31st January 1917

# WAR DIARY
## January 1917.

D.A.D.O.S.
5th Cav Divn
Vol VII

| Jan | 1st | Nothing special to report. |
|---|---|---|
| " | 2nd | do |
| " | 3rd | Ambala Pioneer Battalion left for XIV Corps |
| " | 4th | Secunderabad Pioneer Battalion returned to permanent billets. D.A.D.O.S Conference at Corps H.Q. |
| " | 5th | Nothing special to report. |
| " | 6th | Keys Dummy Signalling received. |
| " | 7th | Visited by A.D.O.S. Cavalry Corps |
| " | 8th | Received 13 Field Forges. Sub. Cond. K. Read left to join 3rd Divisional Artillery |
| " | 9th | Nothing special to report |
| " | 10th | do    do |
| " | 11th | Conference of D.A.D.O.S. at Corps Headquarters |
| " | 12th | Arranged place for I.O.M. at Beauchamps |
| " | 13th | Nothing special to report. |
| " | 14th | 6 Soyer Stoves received. |
| " | 15th | I.O.M. arrived at Beauchamps |
| " | 16th | Visited I.O.M. |
| " | 17th | Visited by A.D.O.S. Cavalry Corps |
| " | 18th | Conference at Corps Headquarters. Received sample Australian jacket |
| " | 19th | Nothing special to report. |

# WAR DIARY
## January 1917.

Jan. 20.     180 pairs of ankle boots were sent to Canadian Pioneer Battalion
" 21     Nothing special to report
" 22     Nothing special to report.
" 23     Acetylene Lamp arrived for trial.
" 24     Nothing special to report
" 25     do
" 26     Received 612 waterproof capes.
" 27     Nothing special to report
" 28     D.A.D.O.S. left for leave to England.
" 29     2 lorries went to Canadian Pioneer Bn. to collect F.S. Boots etc
" 30     Nothing special to report
" 31     do

Douglas White
Capt
D.A.D.O.S
5th Cav. Div.

# WAR DIARY   Vol VIII
## FEBRUARY 1917. D.A.D.O.S. 5th Cav. Divn.

| Feb | 1st | Two carriages Q.F. 13 pdr wired for for B Bty R.C.H.A. |
| --- | --- | --- |
| " | 2nd | Nothing special to report |
| " | 3rd | do do |
| " | 4th | do do |
| " | 5th | Office of D.O.S. moved to G.H.Q. 1st Echelon |
| " | 6th | Two carriages 13pdr for B Bty received |
| " | 7th | Two carriages Q.F. 13pdr wired for for B Bty R.C.H.A. |
| " | 8th | Secunderabad Pioneer Bn. left to join XIII Corps. |
| " | 9th | 71 Bales (852) waterproof coats received. |
| " | 10th | Canadian Pioneer Bn. returned to join their respective units |
| " | 11th | Nothing special to report. |
| " | 12th | do do |
| " | 13th | do do |
| " | 14th | do do |
| " | 15th | Conference at A.D.O.S. Corps H.Q. |
| " | 16th | Nothing special to report |
| " | 17th | Inspected by the General. |

# WAR DIARY

## FEBRUARY 1917.

| Feb | | |
|---|---|---|
| 1st | | Two convoys Q.F. 13 pdr wind for 13 Bty. R.C.H.A. |
| 2nd | | Nothing special to report. |
| 3rd | | do do |
| 4th | | do do |
| 5th | | do do |
| 6th | | Office of D.O.S. moved to G.H.Q. 1st Echelon. |
| 7th | | Two convoys 13pdr for B Bty received. |
| 8th | | Two convoys Q.F. 13pdr wind for 13 Bty R.C.H.A. |
| 9th | | Recommended Prisoner Em. Legel to join XIII Corps. |
| 10th | | 71 Bales (867) Workshop coats received. |
| 11th | | Canadian Prisoner Em. returned to join their respective unit. |
| 12th | | Nothing special to report. |
| 13th | | do do |
| 14th | | do do |
| 15th | | do do |
| 16th | | do do |
| 17th | | Conference at A.D.O.S. Corps H.Q. |
| 18th | | Nothing special to report |
| 19th | | Inspected by the General. 16 bales Hand cuffs received. |

# WAR DIARY
## FEBRUARY 1917

| Feb. | | |
|---|---|---|
| | 18th | Thaw Scheme started late at night. |
| | 19th | 20 Lewis Hand carts received |
| | 20th | New I.O.M. Lieut Patrick took over at Beauchamps. 14 Lewis Hand carts received. |
| | 21st | Nothing Special to report. |
| | 22nd | No Conference at A.D.O.S. Cavalry Corps. |
| | 23rd | 2 Lewis Hand Carts received |
| | 24th | Nothing Special to report |
| | 25th | do do |
| | 26th | do do |
| | 27th | 1352 Swords (British Pattern) received to complete 20th Deccan, 34th Poona and 9th Hodson Horse |
| | 28th | Nothing Special to report |

C Douglas Hubbing Capt
D.A.D.O.S.
5th Cavalry Division

# WAR DIARY DADOS
## MARCH 1917  Vol IX

| | | |
|---|---|---|
| March | 1st | Nothing special to report. Pte J. B. Todd evacuated sick. |
| " | 2nd | British Pattern Swords (488), to complete 18th Lancers, were received |
| " | 3rd | Pte J. Thorne A.O.C. arrived to replace Pte J. B. Todd evacuated sick. |
| " | 4th | Nothing special to report. |
| " | 5th | Hotchkiss gun, to replace unserviceable for 9th Hodsons Horse, received. |
| " | 6th | Nothing special to report |
| " | 7th | 28 Lewis Handcarts received. Fodder Disinfector working at Dargnies |
| " | 8th | Conference of D.A.D.O.S'S at Cavalry Corps |
| " | 9th | Nothing special to report. |
| " | 10 | do |
| " | 11th | do. |
| " | 12th | Private Russell. C.O.C. left this Division for transfer to Canadian Infantry |
| " | 13th | Visited by A.D.O.S Cavalry Corps. Secunderabad Pioneer Battalion returned |
| " | 14 | Secunderabad Pioneer Bn. returned |
| " | 15th | Nothing special to report |

# W.AR. DIARY
## MARCH. 1917.

| | | |
|---|---|---|
| March | 16 | Box respirators small received |
| " | 17 | Balance do do do |
| " | 18 | New Pattern Hotchkiss Packsaddlery received |
| " | 19 | Canadian Cav. Bde moved forward. Evacuating Stores all the day to Senaupont area. |
| " | 20th | The remainder of the Division moved forward less Div H.Q. Motors |
| " | 21st | Moved our Dump to Pont de Metz |
| " | 22nd | |
| " | 23rd | Moved our Dump to Proyart. D.A.D.O.S to Peronne |
| " | 24th | Opened an Advance Dump at Herbécourt. |
| " | 25th | Nothing special to report |
| " | 26th | 5th Cav. Reserve Park rejoined this Division. |
| " | 27th | Nothing special to report |
| " | 28th | do. |
| " | 29th | The Bdes moved back to Cléry Feuillères & Cappy Tents issued to Secunderabad Bde. |

# WAR DIARY
# MARCH 1917

| | |
|---|---|
| March 30 | Divisional H.Q. moved to Villers-Bretonneux & Ambala & Secunderabad Bde to Warfusée & Bayonvillers respectively. Tents collected from Secunderabad Bde. |
| " 31. | Cleared Dump at Proyart & Herbécourt. |

C Douglas-White<br>
Capt<br>
D. A. D. O. S.<br>
5th Cav. Div

# WAR DIARY.
# APRIL 1917.  Vol X

| April | 1st | Nothing special to report. |
|---|---|---|
| " | 2nd | do |
| " | 3rd | do |
| " | 4th | do |
| " | 5th | Received 1500 trench covers from Fourth Army. |
| " | 6th | The whole Division completed with Rangefinders |
| " | 7th | Nothing special to report. |
| " | 8th | Received captured Lewis gun from L.S.H. |
| " | 9th | Division complete with wire-cutters. Re |
| " | 10th | Visited New Area (Meraumont, Tertry, Caulaincourt - Trefcon) & made tent dumps |
| " | 11th | Nothing special to report. |

# APRIL WAR DIARY

| | | |
|---|---|---|
| April | 12 | Nothing special to report |
| " | 13 | do. |
| " | 14 | Moved to Guizancourt. |
| " | 15 | Railhead changed to NESLE. & completed move. |
| " | 16 | Nothing special to report |
| " | 17 | do         do |
| " | 18 | do         do |
| " | 19 | do         do |
| " | 20 | do         do |
| " | 21 | do         do |
| " | 22 | 6000 2nd Blankets received |

CAW

# WAR DIARY
## APRIL 1917

| | | |
|---|---|---|
| April | 23 | Nothing special to report |
| " | 24 | Sub-Conductor Read A.O.C. rejoined my unit |
| " | 25 | Nothing special to report |
| " | 26 | do do |
| " | 27 | do do |
| " | 28 | do do |
| " | 29 | do do |
| " | 30 | do do |

C Douglas Hughes
Capt
D.A.D.O.S
5th Cavalry Division

## WAR DIARY. Vol XI
### MAY 1917

| | | |
|---|---|---|
| May | 1 | Nothing special to report |
| | 2 | do do |
| | 3 | Sergt. Bruce C.O.C. joined from Canadian Corps. |
| | 4 | Nothing special to report |
| | 5 | do do |
| | 6 | do do |
| | 7 | do do |
| | 8 | do do |
| | 9 | do do |
| | 10 | do do |
| | 11 | do do |
| | 12 | do do |
| | 13 | Sent part of Detachment forward to take over New Camp. |

## WAR DIARY
## MAY 1917

| May | 14 | Carried on with our Move. Received 5000 P.H. Helmets |
| --- | --- | --- |
| | 15 | Moved to Nobescourt Farm. |
| | 16 | Nothing special to report |
| | 17 | do do |
| | 18 | Received 300 tents C.S.L & handed over 50 each to 2nd 3rd & 4th Cavalry Divisions. |
| | 19 | 63rd & 89th H.A. Groups, 119th & 221st Siege Batteries, 1/1 London Heavy Bty, H.Q. IV Corps Artillery, 110th, 115th & 125th Heavy Batteries, IV Corps Cav. Regt & Cyclist Battalion, & Corps Siege Park transferred to me |
| | 20 | Came under A.D.O.S. Cavalry Corps. Handed over 100 tents to Cavalry Corps |
| | 21 | Took over 13 tents C.S.L & 262 trench covers from 35th Division |
| | 22 | Handed over 230 trench covers & 8 tents to A.D.O.S. Cavalry Corps |
| | 23 | Railhead changed from Nesle to Roisel |
| | 24 | Took over 190 tents C.S.L & 360 trench covers from 35th Division |
| | 25 | Sent 182 tents & 320 trench covers to A.D.O.S. Cavalry Corps. |
| | 26 | Railhead changed from Roisel to La Chappellette. Moved 16th R.H.A. Bde to 4th Cav. Div |
| | 27 | Handed over 150 Shovels & 8 axes pick to D.A.D.O.S. 59th Division |
| | 28 | Nothing special to report. |

## WAR DIARY
## MAY 1917

| | |
|---|---|
| May 29 | S.C. Read joined O.O. Corps Troops temporarily as Chief Clerk Corps Troops. Lucas Daylight Lamps arrived. |
| 30 | Nothing special to report. |
| 31 | All batteries of Nos 62 & 89 H.A. Group left. Rifles for Grenades arrived 16 per Regt. |

1/6/17.

C Douglas Whi[...]
Capt
D.A.D.O.S.
5th Cavalry Division

## WAR DIARY
## JUNE 1917

| June | | |
|---|---|---|
| | 1 | Nothing special to report |
| | 2 | do |
| | 3 | do |
| | 4 | Nothing special to report. |
| | 5 | Nothing special to report. 2 German Machine guns received |
| | 6 | Nothing special to report. 60 Haversacks arrived - issued 6 tents |
| | 7 | Nothing special to report |
| | 8 | 6 Stretchers Ambulance folding received. |
| | 9 | Visited A.D.O.S. Cavalry Corps. |
| | 10 | 6 Stretchers Ambulance folding received. Anti-Drowning Outfits to complete Div. received |
| | 11 | Nothing special to report. |
| | 12 | 2 German Machine guns received. III Corps Cavalry Regt moved to us. |
| | 13 | Nothing special to report. |
| | 14 | 100 Yukon Packs received. |
| | 15 | Nothing special to report. |
| | 16 | Nothing special to report |

# WAR DIARY
## JUNE 1917

| | | |
|---|---|---|
| June | 17 | Attended Conference re Revised Reserve Pk at Corps H.Q. Visited Reserve Pk in the afternoon to adjust Harness. |
| " | 18 | 9 Hotchkiss guns received for instructional purposes. |
| " | 19 | Nothing special to report. |
| " | 20 | Final adjustment of Reserve Park Harness. |
| " | 21 | Nothing special to report. |
| " | 22 | Issued .9 Hotchkiss guns (1 to each regt) |
| " | 23 | Nothing special to report. |
| " | 24 | A large consignment of gifts from Indian Soldiers Fund. |
| " | 25 | Nothing special to report |
| " | 26 | Reserve Park completed with harness & saddlery. |
| " | 27 | Nothing special to report |
| " | 28 | 1 Wagon L.G.S. (out of 4) received for Reserve Park. |
| " | 29 | Moved camp close to Noberscourt Farm. |
| " | 30 | 3 Wagons L.G.S received to complete Reserve Park |

Douglas Wingo
D.A.D.O.S. Capt
5th Cavalry Division

# WAR DIARY
## July 1917

July 1. Sent pyjamas warm (from Indian Comforts Fund) to Villers-Bretonneux.
" 2.
" 3. Moved Armourer's Shop & part of detachment to Bouvincourt to start Camp.
" 4. Visited A.D.O.S. Cavalry Corps. Obtained 40 tents from 3rd Cav. Div &
" 4. Handed them over to 34th Division at Vraignes.
" 5. Handed over 110 tents to 34th Division 85 at Poeuilly 25 at Vraignes
" 6. Nothing special to report.
" 7. Moved Store to Bouvincourt
" 8. Nothing special to report.
" 9. Moved Office to Bouvincourt.
" 10. Nothing special to report
" 11. Started evacuating Stores.
" 12. Nothing special to report.
" 13. Ambala Bde & Reserve Park + Mhow Field Ambulance moved out of area
" 14. Secunderabad Bde + Canadian Bdes plus Div. H.Q. etc moved out of area

## WAR DIARY
## July 1917.

| | | |
|---|---|---|
| July | 15 | Handed over 237 tents C.S.L to Cavalry Corps & 63 to the Base. Moved Store & office to St. Pol. |
| July | 16 | Div. H.Q. opened at St. Pol |
| " | 17 | Ambala & Canadian Bdes arrived in their new area |
| " | 18 | Secunderabad Bde arrived in its new area |
| " | 19 | Received 50 tents C.S.L from Cavalry Corps |
| " | 20 | Secunderabad Bde moved their area |
| " | 21 | Canadian Bde H.Q. moved to Warrans |
| " | 22 | Nothing special to report |
| " | 23 | do do |
| " | 24 | do do |
| " | 25 | do do |
| " | 26 | Cleared the Ordnance Dump at Villers-Bretonneux |

# WAR DIARY
## July. 1917.

July 27 — ~~Nothing special to report~~ All Batteries & Ammunition Column (less S.A.A. Sect¹) moved to Canadian Camp

" 28 — Delivered Stores to Batteries

" 29 — Nothing special to report

" 30 — "      "      "      "

" 31 — Moved to Henchin

31/7/17.

C Douglas Why
Capt
D.A.D.O.S
5th Cavalry Division

WAR DIARY
August 1917

| Aug | 1 | Nothing special to report |
| " | 2 | Visited A.D.O.S. Cavalry Corps |
| " | 3 | Nothing special to report. |
| " | 4 | I.O.M inspected XIV Bty H |
| " | 5 | Nothing special to report. |
| " | 6 | Visited by the A.D.O.S. |
| " | 7 | Nothing special to report |
| " | 8 | do do |
| " | 9 | do do |
| " | 10 | do do |
| " | 11 | do do |
| " | 12 | do do |

# WAR DIARY

| | | |
|---|---|---|
| Aug | 13 | Nothing special to report |
| " | 14 | do |
| " | 15 | do |
| " | 16 | do |
| " | 17 | D.A.D.O.S. proceeded on leave to England |
| " | 18 | Pte J. Graves A.O.C. left to join 3rd Cavalry Division |
| " | 19 | Nothing special to report |
| " | 20 | One gun carriage 13pdr received for A Bty. R.C.H.A. |
| " | 21 | Nothing special to report |
| " | 22 | do         do |
| " | 23 | do         do |
| " | 24 | do         do |
| " | 25 | One gun carriage 13pdr received for X Bty R.H.A. |
| " | 26 | One water cart received for X Bty R.H.A. |
| " | 27 | D.A.D.O.S. returned from leave in England |

# WAR DIARY
## AUGUST 1917

| Aug | 28 | Nothing special to report |
| " | 29 | do                do |
| " | 30 | do                do |
| " | 31 | One gun Q.F 13pdr received for N Bty. |

1/9/17.

C Douglas White
Capt
D.A.D.O.S
5th Cavalry Division

www.ingramcontent.com/pod-product-compliance
Lightning Source LLC
Chambersburg PA
CBHW081250170426
43191CB00037B/2112